Introduc

The Llŷn Peninsula, with a line of volca
extends westwards from Snowdonia to the
its tip overlooking Bardsey Island (Ynys Enlli), ...age.
Its stunning varied Heritage Coast falls within a (... of Outstanding
Natural Beauty, some owned by the National Tust. A predominantly Welsh
speaking area, the Llŷn has welcomed generations of visitors.

Its rugged cliffs, rocky headlands, sheltered estuaries and coves, dunes, and sandy beaches provide numerous habitats for wildlife. Inland are hedged fields, small hills, narrow lanes, and small traditional family farms. Former fishing villages such as Abersoch, Aberdaron and Nefyn that have produced generations of seafarers, are now popular tourist destinations, with the south coast attracting sailing and watersport enthusiasts. Running around the length of the peninsula is the waymarked Wales Coast Path, which opened in 2012, giving access to the breathtaking coastline.

Occupied since pre-historic times, the isolation of the Llŷn attracted early Christians, whose Celtic Church survived until the 13thC. The beautiful landscape offers great historical interest, including one of Britain's most spectacular Iron Age hillforts and small churches on the ancient Pilgrim coastal routes to Bardsey.

The Llŷn's unique landscape is best explored on foot to appreciate its beautiful scenery, wildlife and history. The 30 walks in this revised and updated second edition of my book cover the spectacular coast, incorporating the best sections of the Wales Coast Path, as well as the peninsula's low and high hills, offering panoramic views.

The routes, which range from an easy 2¼ mile cliff-top walk to a challenging 9 mile exploration of hills and moorland, follow public rights of way or permissive paths and visit designated Open Access land. Most routes, as well as containing shorter walk options, can easily be linked with others, to provide longer day walks, if required.

Walking boots are recommended, along with appropriate clothing to protect against the elements. Remember that the condition of paths can vary according to season and weather. The Wales Coast Path is also subject to further improvements. Please refer any problems encountered to Gwynedd Council Rights of Way (www.gwynedd.gov.uk or 01758 704091).

Each walk has a detailed map and description which enables the route to be followed without difficulty. Bear in mind though that changes in detail can occur at any time – eg. new stiles/gates, path diversions and so on. The location of each walk is shown on the back cover and a summary of their key features is also given. This includes an estimated walking time, but allow more time to enjoy the scenery and sights.

Please observe the country code and take particular care not to damage any ancient site visited. *Enjoy your walking!*

CRICCIETH TO LLANYSTUMDWY

DESCRIPTION A 5½ mile walk (**A**) combining coast and countryside. The route follows the Coast Path to join the Afon Dwyfor, then heads inland to Llanystumdwy, where refreshments and the David Lloyd George Museum await, before returning via quiet country lane, tracks and bridleways. Allow about 3 hours. The route includes alternative shorter 2¾ mile (**B**) or 2¼ mile (**C**) walks, with other options easily devised. It can easily be extended to 6¾ mile walk, by incorporating Walk 2.

START Car park beneath Criccieth Castle just above the western beach. SH 499377.

DIRECTIONS The castle is signposted from the A497 at the western end of Criccieth. Follow the road past an alternative beach car park to one beneath the castle.

*C*riccieth Castle, *standing on a hill overlooking the sea, was built by Llywelyn the Great about 1230, and later enlarged by his grandson, Llywelyn ap Gruffudd. By 1283 it was under English control, after which it was strengthened by Edward I to serve as one of his chain of castles after his conquest of Wales. In 1404, it was captured and burned by Owain Glyndŵr's rebels and remained a ruin.*

I Follow the road down and on above the beach. Shortly, follow the signposted Coast Path along a pathway above the promenade past the alternative car park – *enjoying extensive views across Cardigan Bay* – to an information board. Continue along the stony Coast Path to a gate beyond a house. Keep ahead, soon bending past a modern house. Turn LEFT and follow the enclosed Coast Path to the bend of a track. (For **Walks B/C**, turn right along the track. For **Walk C**, on the bend, cross a stone stile. Keep ahead, turn right through a gap in the boundary, follow a path through trees then bear right along a field edge to a hidden kissing gate. Follow the hedge-lined path to a ladder-stile just beyond a gate on the left. Cross the field to another ladder-stile to join the main route. For **Walk B**, continue on the track, then cross the railway line. Follow the enclosed path past a house and outbuilding. Go up an access track to the A497. Turn right along the pavement opposite to rejoin the main route at point 4.)

2 Follow the path just above the beach, briefly near the track, past a finger post and on along a green track, which curves to a low headland – *offering views to Criccieth and Snowdonia.* The track gradually becomes an enclosed path passing above the pebbly shore. The path then bends inland near the Afon Dwyfor to a kissing gate on its bend and follows the river to another kissing gate. Go along the field edge and through a further kissing gate. Turn RIGHT with the Coast Path along the edge of a long field, then an enclosed track to a gate and on over the railway line (heed warnings). Continue along the track to Aberkin Farm, pass through small gates and between buildings, then follow its driveway past farm buildings to the A497.

3 Cross the road to a finger post opposite, where you leave the Coast Path. Go through the nearby small gate and follow a track past houses to the road in Llanystumdwy. (To visit the the David Lloyd George museum turn right). Take the road opposite signposted to Ty Newydd and follow it out of the village. After ¾ mile go through the gated entrance to Broneifion Farm on the right, by a stone house. Follow the wooded access track past side tracks, Y Gweithdy/Dwyfor cottages and the entrance to Drws y Coed. Continue down past a large walled garden to join the driveway leading from Bron Eifion Hotel, which you follow down to the A497. Turn LEFT along the pavement.

4 Shortly at an old milestone cross the road with care to Tan Lon lodge opposite. Go down the access lane by an adjoining road, then follow a stony track to pass under the railway line and up to a finger post opposite a ladder-stile. (By continuing on the track you can rejoin the Coast Path if you want.) Turn LEFT along the delightful hedge-lined bridleway, through a gate and on between cottages to follow the leafy access drive to the road. Follow it RIGHT down to the start.

WALK 2

AFON DWYFOR

DESCRIPTION An enjoyable 3 mile walk from Llanystumdwy, the village associated with David Lloyd George, that can be combined with a visit to the museum dedicated to him. The walk follows a delightful section of woodland path near the Afon Dwyfor, before returning by minor roads and field paths. Allow about 1½ hours.

START Llanystumdwy. SH 475384.

DIRECTIONS Llanystumdwy lies just off the A497 west of Criccieth, where there is a car park or roadside parking.

David Lloyd George (1863-1945), in spite of his colourful private life, is considered a Welsh genius, one of the greatest statesmen of the 20thC. He grew up in a cottage in Llanystumdwy and is buried in the village. He served as a Liberal MP for Caernarfon (1890-1945, Chancellor between 1906-14, and Prime Minister 1916-22). A charismatic and controversial figure who laid the foundations for the Welfare State.

1 Go through the village past the David Lloyd George museum, then just before the bridge over the river, take the minor road on the right signposted to Ty Newydd. At the end of terraced cottages, take a signposted path on the left angling down through the trees, passing beneath a commemorative monument to David Lloyd George, to a small gate. Now follow the delightful gated wooded riverside path, past a footbridge, for 1¼ miles to emerge onto a minor road.

2 Follow the road RIGHT to its end at Trefan farm. Turn LEFT along a track past the end of farm buildings to a gate. Go along a short section of enclosed track to another gate, then along a field edge to a kissing gate. Go along the edge of the next field to an old kissing gate in the corner and through the garden past Cefn y Main cottage. Follow the driveway to a minor road. Follow it RIGHT back to Llanystumdwy.

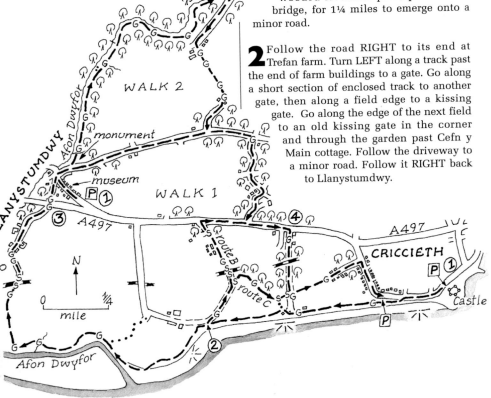

WALK 3

CARN FADRYN & GARN BACH

DESCRIPTION A 3⅓ mile walk (**A**) featuring the distinctive heather and rock covered hill of Carn Fadryn, (1216 feet/371 metres), with its Iron Age hillfort and extensive views of the Llŷn, as well as the nearby hill of Garn Bach (921 feet/281 metres), both designated Open Access areas. Although not high, Carn Fadryn is mountainous in character, but a delightful meandering path makes for an enjoyable ascent. Avoid in poor visibility. Allow about 2½ hours. Also included is 3 mile walk (**B**) around the lower slopes of Carn Fadryn, which can be combined with an ascent of both tops.
START Old Chapel, Garnfadryn. SH 278345.
DIRECTIONS Garnfadryn lies south of Morfa Nefyn. There is a car park by the former chapel.

On the summit of Carn Fadryn is an Iron Age walled hillfort containing stone huts, and a small fort reputedly built by Roderic and Maelgwyn, the sons of Owain Gwynedd in the 12thC.

1 From the end of the chapel house go up an enclosed access track. When it bends right follow a path up to a gate by a small covered reservoir beneath Carn Fadryn. Turn RIGHT along the path near the boundary, soon rising steadily to reach a viewpoint looking east to nearby Pwllheli and the distant mountains of Snowdonia. The path then angles away from the wall. (For **Walk B** continue beside the wall to cross a stile in it and resume text at point 3.) The path meanders steadily up the southern slopes of Carn Fadryn, changing in character from wide short cut grass to stone stepped. Eventually the path passes through the lower stone ramparts of the hillfort to reach it flattish interior.

2 There are a choice of three paths to the summit trig point as shown. The clearest follows cairns through the centre of the fort. I suggest that you follow a sketchy path to follow the nearby small craggy heather western ridge to the trig point – *offering superb views along both coasts of the Llŷn, and to the Snowdonia mountains.* Return briefly down the path, then follow another path towards the fort's flat centre to pass a large cairn to reach another. Follow the clear path south to rejoin your ascent path. Descend the hillside, then just before the final bend, take another path angling LEFT down to cross a stile in the wall below.

3 Go across open pasture towards a kissing gate ahead, then bear LEFT along a path, soon joining another, which you follow down to cross a waymarked stone stile just to the left of a gate in the wall ahead – *with new views east.* (For **Walk B** cross the nearby ladder-stile. Turn RIGHT briefly alongside the fence, then angle away across upland pasture to pass through a gap in the old wall ahead. Go up the next field to join the wall ahead where it meets an old low boundary. Follow the wall up to pass a nearby small crag offering superb views, then down the steep slope to cross a ladder-stile over it. Go half-RIGHT across the large field to the wall ahead. Follow it LEFT, soon through reeds then bracken to a stile. Go along the next field edge to another stile. Now follow the wall along the forest edge (bracken in high summer) to a post on the wall where you cross a stone stile into the second adjoining field. Cross the nearby stile. Now follow the wall through two fields (stiles) past Coed Garn Fadryn and across bracken-covered pasture to its corner. Go past the nearby ruin to join a green track. After passing a cottage it rises beneath the western slopes of Carn Fadryn, later joining a road, which continues up to a junction. Keep ahead back to the start.)

For **Walk A** turn RIGHT and follow the wall up to the craggy top of Garn Bach. Follow a path to the next small rocky top, then down the part rock-covered slope near the wall to go through a waymarked small iron gate in it above Pen-y-Caerau cottage. Go along its access track, then lane past cottages – all the way to the village road for a simple return if preferred.

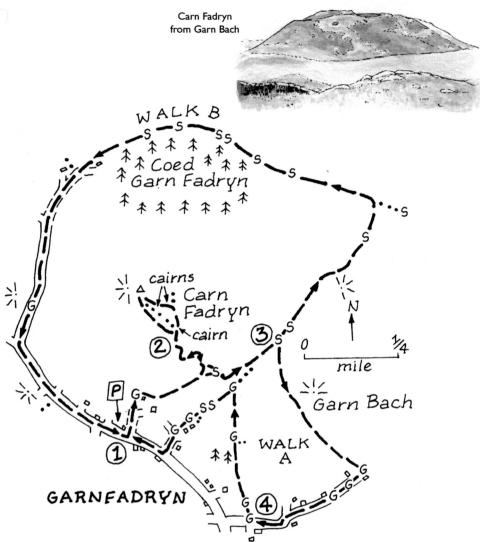

Carn Fadryn
from Garn Bach

WALK B

Coed
Garn Fadryn

cairns
Carn Fadryn
cairn

② ③

cairn

P G

N

0   ¼
mile

Garn Bach

WALK A

① ④

GARNFADRYN

4 At a farm entrance, go through a kissing gate on the right. Follow the path along the edge of two small fields to a small gate. Continue along the next field edge and up a faint green track. Soon leave it to walk alongside the perimeter fence of a small wood, then follow a waymarked path ahead to a kissing gate and on beside an old wall. At its corner continue ahead up the long field to a kissing gate in the wall ahead seen on your outward route. Turn LEFT to follow a path down across bracken covered pasture. After about 70 yards continue down its right fork to cross two stiles in a recessed boundary corner ahead. Go down the enclosed path to a waymarked gate and down the left-hand edge of two fields to a kissing gate, then follow an access track down to the village road. Turn RIGHT back to the start.

5

WALK 4

AROUND MYNYTHO COMMON

DESCRIPTION A 3¾ mile walk (**A**) linking three distinctive low hills near Mynytho, featuring one of the area's distinctive landmarks – the remains of an old windmill, known locally as the 'jam pot' – and extensive views. Allow about 2 hours. The route can be shortened to a 2¼ mile walk (**B**).
START Car park/picnic area, Mynytho. SH 303311.
DIRECTIONS Heading west on the B4413 out of Mynytho, go past the road leading to the school to find a car park/picnic area/toilets by the next road on the right just before the speed derestriction signs.

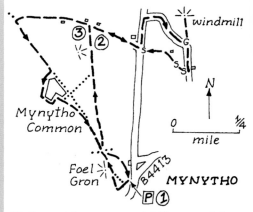

I From the near end of the picnic table area, take an initially stepped path angling across Foel Gron, soon bending right up through heather and bracken to reach its summit cairn for superb all-round views – *including the Rivals, Abersoch and distant Snowdonia*. The path now descends the northern slopes to a cross a stony access track. Take the wide path ahead near the wall (not narrow green track-your return route), soon narrowing and rising steadily across Mynytho Common – *a traditionally important local source of firewood and heather for roofing material or brooms*. It then levels out and continues beside the wall to an access track by a cottage. (For **Walk B** turn left and resume text at paragraph 3.)

2 Follow the track RIGHT to a minor road. Turn LEFT, then take a side road round to a kissing gate giving access to National Trust owned Foel Felin Wynt. After visiting the former windmill on the summit, continue down the road. At a house cross a stile on the right. Angle across the field corner to cross a stile amongst trees and on to an ivy-covered stone ruin. Here, bear LEFT across the field past a telegraph pole to a stile onto the road. Go along your outward track opposite.

3 Go past the cottage and follow a path by the wall down past a gate to a cross-path. Follow it LEFT steadily rising. At a junction of narrow green tracks by the corner of a fenced enclosure corner, turn RIGHT. Follow the track round near the enclosure boundary then a wider track heading towards Foel Gron to rejoin your outward route. Go up the path back onto Foel Gron. On the first bend, turn LEFT along another path, soon descending and passing above the school to reach the toilets/car park.

WALK 5

MYNYDD TIR-Y-CWMWD

DESCRIPTION A 2½ mile walk (**A**) around the attractive rocky headland of Mynydd Tir-y-Cwmwd and onto its summit (436 feet/133 metres) for extensive all-round views. You have an initial choice of ascents to the Iron Man sculpture on Mynydd Tir-y-Cwmwd: **Route a** follows a new section of the Coast Path to Plas Glyn-y-Weddw and up through woodland. **Route b** climbs from the beach, inaccessible at high tide, via a steep railed stepped path. Allow about 1½ hours. Included is a 2¼ mile walk (**B**) that omits the summit.
START National Trust beach car park, Llanbedrog. SH 331315.
DIRECTIONS The large car park is just past the church.

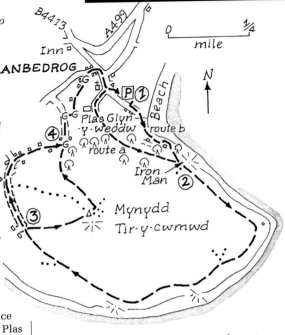

Mynydd Tir-y-Cwmwd *overlooks to the north a sheltered sandy beach and bay which once provided good anchorage, from where, in the early 19thC boats sailed regularly to South Wales, Liverpool and Dublin. St. Pedrog, a Welsh saint, established a church here in the 6thC. The current church dates from the 13thC. Nearby is Plas Glyn-y-Weddw, a dower house built in 1856 by Lady Love Jones Parry. In 1896 it became an art gallery and a ballroom. A horse-tramway was also extended along the sandhills from Pwllheli to the hall's entrance. Until 1927, when it closed, trips by tram to Llanbedrog beach and to the house for dances and afternoon teas, were popular with holidaymakers. The restored hall is now run by a trust as an art gallery (open daily 10.00-17.00, closed Tues outside school holidays), with a café.*

| **Route a**: From the car park entrance follow the signposted Coast Path up Plas Glyn-y-Weddw's driveway opposite. Go past the hall then follow a surfaced path past the car park entrance and John Andrews Theatre, then a wide stony path up through mature woodland. After seats a stepped path rises more steeply through woodland. At a bench and finger post continue up the stone path through trees to join the ascending path from the beach.

Route b: At the far end of the car park, descend to the road by toilets, and follow it to the beach. Cross a stream and head towards a white cottage amongst woodland. Pass in front of Foxhole and follow a lane above the shore, then descend steps to pass in front of The Boathouse. Just beyond take the steep stepped railed path, signposted to Mynydd Tir-y-cwmwd, up the tree covered slope, shortly joined by the Coast Path.

2 At the top turn LEFT to the Iron Man sculpture at a good viewpoint then continue at the waymarked Coast Path along the north-eastern side of the headland, later bending south-west and passing side paths – *soon with views across to Abersoch, Mynydd Cilan and St Tudwal's Islands. The path then bends inland and rises.* At a waymark post, where the Coast Path turns left, continue with the path ahead.

3 Soon after passing a seat and before a nearby house's access track you have a choice. (For **Walk B** continue down the stony track, then a lane. Turn right behind Bronwydd along an access track to Gulls' Way, then follow a path to a wood edge. Turn left down a path to a small gate at point 4.) For **Walk A** turn RIGHT up a path to the summit trig point and stone cairn. Pass between seats at the western side of the cairn and follow a path through heather, gorse & bracken towards Llanbedrog, descending to a wall corner, then through trees to a small gate.

4 Go past a cottage and along a track. Shortly, turn RIGHT through a small gate and go along the field edge to a kissing gate. Turn LEFT down the next long field edge, past a cottage, to a small gate. Turn RIGHT down the road beyond. At the junction turn RIGHT then follow the road ahead past the church back to the start.

WALK 6
ABERSOCH – MYNYTHO

DESCRIPTION A varied 7 mile walk exploring the coast and countryside north of Abersoch. It features a 1½ mile section of delightful beach between Abersoch and the headland of Mynydd Tir-y-cwmwd and the adjoining countryside inland as far as Mynytho, where you pass an ancient well. Allow about 4 hours. Plan to complete the beach section at low tide.

START Abersoch SH 313282, A499 roadside parking opposite Tywyn y fach SH 315291 or beach car park beneath Mynydd Tir-y-cwmwd SH 329303.

DIRECTIONS The alternative beach car park is accessed via a minor road off the A499 just outside Llanbedrog.

*A*bersoch *is a popular tourist and water-sports resort, with a beach and small harbour. It is located in St Tudwal's Road – a large sheltered bay which provided good anchorage for ships. It was once said that the whole of the British Fleet could safely anchor in the bay, now it is home to a flotilla of pleasure craft. Nearby are two islands, named after St Tudwal, a 6thC saint from Brittany, the larger containing the remains of a 12thC priory.*

I Leave Abersoch on the A499, crossing over the river, which forms a small harbour as it heads towards the sea. Go past a road on the left by Abersoch Land and Sea Business. Opposite a post box and bus stop is a wide access to the beach. Alternatively follow the road further to where the signposted Coast Path passes through National Trust owned Tywyn y fach into the dunes. Head along the beach towards the majestic headland of Mynydd Tir-y-cwmwd. At the last of the beach bungalows beneath the crags of Mynydd Tir-y-cwmwd leave the beach to reach a car park.

2 Continue with the Coast Path along the minor road to where the signposted Coast Path rises onto Mynydd Tir-y-cwmwd opposite the entrance to Garreg Fawr. Just beyond take a signposted path on the left down towards a caravan park and on to a small gate. Go past a cottage and along its access track to the bend of a minor road. Go up the shady right fork to rejoin the beach road. Follow it up past Geufron cottage. Shortly, take a signposted path down the driveway of Pen y Gors, then turn LEFT at the garage and follow a courtesy path past the property. A path then descends through trees to the A499. Turn RIGHT along the pavement past the entrance to Glynllifon.

3 At the house on the bend, cross the road with care to follow a signposted path up a stony track opposite through woodland. After 40 yards angle RIGHT to a kissing gate and follow a path beside the stream up to a small iron gate. Go across the gated driveway and follow the path past the garage and up steps to a small iron gate. The path now rises past gorse, then briefly accompanies a fence on your right. At its corner angle RIGHT to cross an old boundary amongst trees. Now follow a path through gorse, then go up its left fork through more gorse and bracken to a solitary old gatepost ahead at a waymarked boundary corner – *with a view of the old hill-top windmill, known locally as the 'jam pot'.* Follow the boundary on your left to a small raised iron gate, then go along Erw's garden edge and up its driveway. Turn RIGHT along the lane.

4 On the bend, at the entrance to Bodwrog caravan site, go along the delightful hedge-lined wide green path ahead to a kissing gate. Continue along an access track to a junction with a road. Turn LEFT and at the next junction RIGHT. Later, at small cross-roads, turn LEFT on a signposted path down a lane past nearby Horeb chapel. On the bend – *nearby to the left is the ancient well of Ffynnon Fyw* – turn RIGHT on the way-marked path (can be wet in places). After about 70 yards it bends half-LEFT, then continues south-west across an area of rough common to the bend of a track. Go ahead

8

to Llanbedrog

along the track to a road by houses. Follow it LEFT, and at a minor junction by a small stone building go down the access track ahead past a house.

shop

MYNYTHO

well

Abersoch Harbour

Mynydd
Tir-y-cwmwd

link to
walk 5

N

0   ¼
mile

Dunes

Tywyn
y fâch

A499

ABERSOCH

ahead beside a fence at the bottom of a small hill, shortly bending down to a kissing gate and sleeper bridge. Follow a path along the bottom of the attractive valley to eventually reach a kissing gate. Follow the path over the small rise ahead, then on past two nearby privately developed small lakes and on through trees to a stile. Keep ahead along the edge of a small wooded valley and at a waymarked telegraph pole bear LEFT up to pass through a gap in gorse/bramble. Keep ahead towards houses, cross sleeper bridges in a boggy area and continue to a stile hidden by gorse in the descending boundary ahead. The path rises through bracken, then goes along the bottom field edge to a kissing gate on the right. Descend the stepped path through trees, then follow an access track to the A499 in Abersoch. Turn RIGHT back to the start.

5 As it bends left keep ahead on the way-marked path through trees. After a kissing gate, the path descends gently to cross a stream and a farm track, then continues

PORTH CEIRIAD

DESCRIPTION A 6 mile walk from Abersoch following the Coast Path south to Porth Ceiriad, with its fine beach, then a countryside return. The walk includes a splendid new 1¾ mile section of cliff-top path, offering close views of St Tudwal's islands. Allow about 3½ hours.

START Beach car park, Abersoch. SH 314277.

DIRECTIONS Head south along the main street. Where the one-way system turns right, continue ahead then take the first road on the left by the Wylfa Hotel down to the large car park (fee payable).

See **Walk 6** *for information on Abersoch.*

1 You have an initial choice of beach (**a**) and (**b**) routes south to the entrance to another beach car park with toilets at point 2, according to the tide.
For **route a** follow the lane to the slipway and head south along the beach. At the last of chalets leave the beach by a small slipway. For **route b** from the car park entrance follow the signposted Coast Path along the road to the golf club, then continue on a rough track (a bridleway) across the golf course.

2 Follow the signposted Coast Path up the road, then shortly LEFT along a lane. After passing dwellings, continue along a stony track above the shore. At The Old Lifeboat House the track bends inland and rises steadily. Just beyond Nyth y Mor cottage go through a kissing gate on the left. Follow the fenced stony Coast Path past an old engine house to a small gate. The Coast Path now rises RIGHT and continues along the part gorse covered cliffs, then angles down to a fence corner – *offering extensive views around Cardigan Bay.* The wide path continues parallel with the fence. *Nearby are St Tudwal's islands. One has a lighthouse, built in 1877, automated in 1922, and converted to solar power in 1995. The other contains the remains of a 12thC priory.* The Coast Path follows the embanked fence southwards, later passing closer to the cliff edge, after which it rises and continues near the fence.

3 When the fence bends inland keep ahead to descend to a large footbridge over a stream, which tumbles into the clear sea as Pistyll Cim. The path now climbs steadily alongside a new fence. At its corner – *with a great view looking across Porth Ceriad towards Mynydd Gilan headland* – the path bends north west to a kissing gate/gates. It then descends – *with a good view along the beach* – and continues along the cliffs to another kissing gate into National Trust land. The nearby kissing gate gives access to Porth Ceiriad's beach. Follow a wide path angling RIGHT to a waymarked path junction. Bear LEFT along the Coast Path, soon rising and bending inland, parallel with a nearby track. The path rises steadily to a kissing gate onto a minor road by Nant-y-Big. Continue along the road.

4 Shortly, go through a small metal gate on the right opposite Ceiriad cottage. Head half-RIGHT across the field then follow the fence to a gate in the corner onto a waymarked path junction. Follow the path rising LEFT and continuing between boundaries to cross a substantial stile. Ignore the adjoining stile but continue ahead along the edge of two fields (stiles) then turn RIGHT through gates. Follow the track to a gate by farm buildings, then angle RIGHT to follow a waymarked path past a house to a hidden kissing gate on the left. Go down a gorse enclosed path to cross a stile. Go along the field edge and through an old gateway by a waymark post. Turn LEFT and follow the field edge round to a kissing gate. Go past a house to another kissing gate onto a driveway to reach a nearby road. Go briefly along the road, then turn LEFT down a single track road by a chapel. After an old farmhouse the hedge/tree-lined lane becomes narrow and steadily descends. After a staggered junction, continue down the rough track to the golf course. Now either follow a track through the golf course, then road back to the start, or continue ahead to access the beach for a return to the slipway, dependent on your initial outward route.

WALK 8
ABERSOCH

DESCRIPTION A 2¾ mile walk around Abersoch's headland, then south along the beach at low tide, returning through the golf course. Allow about 1½ hours. The route can be joined at various places and undertaken as two shorter walks.
START As Walk 7.

Go back up the road, then turn RIGHT along the main street to crossroads by Londis stores. Follow the road ahead round to pass above a small jetty at the outer harbour. After passing Lon Rhoslyn continue up the no through road. At its end by Cilfach Coed, go down a railed stepped path to pass beneath a house and along its narrow access track. Go across a small parking area, then follow a path to a good viewpoint. Head RIGHT across the large car park, then go down the road. On the bend turn LEFT through another car park with café, then walk south along the beach past chalets to a slipway/café. Continue along the beach, then at the last of chalets go along a small slipway to the entrance to a beach car park with toilets.

2 Turn RIGHT and follow a track through the golf course to the golf club, then its access road to the car park entrance.

Porth Ceiriad

WALK 9
MYNYDD CILAN

DESCRIPTION A delightful 3¾ mile (**A**) or 3¼ mile (**B**) walk around the attractive headland of Mynydd Cilan, part owned by the National Trust. The route follows the Coast Path around the headland, returning by a choice of routes. Walk A continues further with the Coast Path. Walk B completes the circuit of Open Access land. Allow about 2½ hours.

START Mynydd Cilan National Trust car park. SH 295247.

DIRECTIONS From Abersoch follow the road south to Sarn Bach. Continue with the road signposted to Cilan, later rising and passing an old chapel. Just past a no through road sign, turn right by Erw Deg bungalow along a lane which ends at cottages and the grass car park.

1 Follow the track ahead past Ty Newydd cottage then take the right fork, shortly descending. When it splits again keep ahead. At Pen y Groes cottage turn LEFT, past a ruin, then go up a green track ahead. Cross a track leading to Garreg Haul. At the boundary corner turn RIGHT past a small lilly pond. Follow the path towards Porth Neigwl. At a waymark post turn LEFT and follow the Coast Path along the headland, soon bending left to a crossroad of paths. Here turn RIGHT and continue with the wide path, shortly passing a boundary corner, then rising alongside the boundary. Go up either fork to the trig point by a small underground reservoir. Continue on the delightful path, soon bending south-east and splitting, then rejoining. Keep with the wide path, shortly splitting again then rejoining. It then descends towards the sea at the tip of the headland, before bending LEFT past a waymark post and rising.

2 At a waymark post by a facing old iron gate you have a choice: For **Walk A**, turn RIGHT down the Coast Path beside the boundary to go through the right of two kissing gates. Continue along the cliffs, soon descending past a stile – *enjoying extensive views to Porth Ceiriad and across Cardigan*

Bay – to a small gate. The path continues north between fences down to a small gate. After a footbridge it bends inland up to a kissing gate, then rises to another kissing gate. Don't follow a new section of the Coast Path along the cliffs to Porth Ceiriad, but continue up a field to a large gate. Follow the boundary up to a kissing gate. Go across the next field to a kissing gate near Muriau, then follow its access track to the road. Follow it RIGHT, then at Erw Deg, follow the lane back to the start.

For **Walk B**, turn LEFT up and along the wide path beside the boundary, soon becoming a narrow green track. Go past the boundary corner. When the track splits, with the left fork heading towards a small lake, continue along the right fork past a nearby small reedy pool and on to join an access track from the nearby white house. After 10 yards, take a path angling RIGHT across another access track, then past another small reedy pool to go through a wide gap in the far boundary corner. Turn LEFT along an enclosed bridleway, then follow a stony track past 1 Parc y Brennin to join another wide track to reach the entrance to Mynydd Cilan.

WALK 10
PORTH NEIGWL

DESCRIPTION A 3¾ mile walk (**A**) from Porth Neigwl (Hell's Mouth), which has witnessed many shipwrecks. The route follows the Coast Path along the popular sandy beach at low tide or along the low cliffs to Mynydd Cilan headland. It then follows paths inland to the ancient village of Llanengan, with its 15thC church and inviting country inn. Allow about 2½ hours. A shorter 2¾ mile walk (**B**) is included and combining beach and cliff-top path makes a simple 2 mile walk. It can also easily be extended to combine with Walk 11.

START Porth Neigwl National Trust car park. SH 284267.

DIRECTIONS From Abersoch head to Llanengan and continue to the car park.

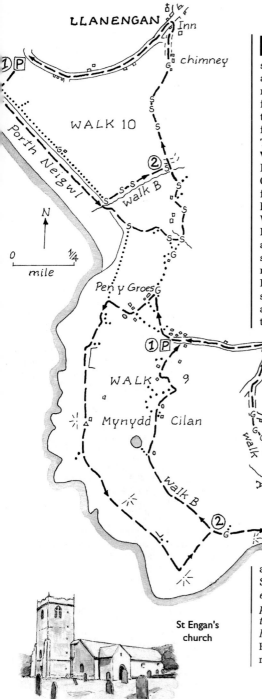

LLANENGAN

Inn

chimney

WALK 10

Porth Neigwl

② walk B

N

0 ¼
mile

Pen y Groes

①P

WALK 9

Mynydd Cilan

walk A

walk B

②

St Engan's
church

■ Follow the path to Porth Neigl, then walk along the beach. Alternatively follow the signposted Coast Path through dunes and along the low cliffs. (For **Walk B**, after ¾ miles just before a stream cross a stile in a fence on the cliffs, then follow a path over two further stiles, and across the next large field to cross a ladder-stile in the corner. Turn left and resume text at point 2) For **Walk A** after crossing the stream go to a large waymark post upon the low cliffs. Continue along the cliffs to a stile into a field. Here you leave the Coast Path, which heads up onto Mynydd Cilan – a link to Walk 11. Instead, follow a wide path angling LEFT through a field, then a stony track up across the hillside. Just after it bends up sharp right follow a path ahead, past a waymark post and down to cross a stile. Head LEFT on a permissive path to cross another stile, then a stream. Go up the slope ahead and bear LEFT up through gorse. Go across the field to a waymark post amongst gorse above the farm and on to cross a stile. Head down towards a house, then turn RIGHT along the lower track. Cross a stile on the left, go along the field edge, over a footbridge and past the nearby ladder-stile.

2 Continue beside the fence and on beneath the small rocky ridge to a stile. Go along the next field to cross a stile and another ahead, then follow the boundary towards a hilltop chimney – *that served a local lead-mine in the 19thC* – to gates beyond an ivy covered ruin. Keep ahead to join the nearby house's access track. When it bends left go along a shady track ahead to the Sun Hotel in Llanengan. Visit St Engan's church. *It stands on the site of an earlier 6thC church and remains a popular place for pilgrimage en route to Bardsey. In the churchyard is Ffynnon Engan, said to have healing properties.* Return to the Sun Hotel, then after refreshments follow the road back to the start.

MYNYDD Y GRAIG & MYNYDD PENARFYNYDD

DESCRIPTION A 4½ mile walk (**A**) from Rhiw exploring two attractive Open Access upland areas above the sea owned by the National Trust. Mynydd y Graig (793 feet/242 metres), with its Iron Age hillfort of Creigiau Gwineu, and Penarfynydd (580 feet/177 metres) offer delightful walking on good paths and extensive views. Allow about 2½ hours. A shorter 2½ mile circuit of Mynydd y Graig (**B**) is included. Near the village is Plas yn Rhiw, a restored 16thC manor house and gardens owned by the National Trust – well worth a visit.

START Y Rhiw. SH 227280.

DIRECTIONS On the bend of the B4413 by the chapel in Botwnnog, take the minor road signposted to Y Rhiw. Take the third turning on the left after nearly 2 miles. Follow the road up to its highest point (start of Walk 12). Continue down the road to reach a junction in Y Rhiw. Turn left to find limited roadside parking opposite Neuadd y rhiw, the village hall.

Y Rhiw, standing at over 600 feet, is the highest village on Llŷn, lying in an area that has been occupied since prehistoric times. Originally a small farming and fishing community, it became associated with the mining of manganese, after its discovery here in 1827. In the 1840s 50 men were involved, with donkeys taking ore down to Porth Cadlan for loading onto small vessels. After years of subsequent decline, mining boomed in the early 20thC with the area becoming the main UK producer of manganese, at its peak employing around 200 men. Ore was taken from a jetty at nearby Porth Ysgo by boat to Liverpool and London. During the two World Wars it was used for the strengthening of steel. The last mine closed in 1945.

1 Take the nearby signposted path opposite Llys Hyfryd. Follow it down an access track, then go through a waymarked gate on the right just before a house. Follow the boundary on the left round and along the edge of another field – *with a view ahead of the small rocky ridge of Mynydd y Graig* – to a stile in the corner and on to a kissing gate ahead onto a road. Turn RIGHT and take the signposted Coast Path LEFT between cottages. Continue along a track/lane to go through a gate into National Trust land. Just beyond turn RIGHT and follow a wide path near the wall up to reach a facing stone stile.

2 Here turn LEFT up a path alongside the wall to a ladder-stile onto Mynydd y Graig. After visiting the nearby summit for all-round views, continue southwards on a clear path, gradually descending and passing a small collapsed concrete building to reach a small rocky top. Work your way with care down its eastern seaward side to join a visible path below which leads to the other rocky top of Graig Fawr ahead. Descend its western side to a wide path and a small gate in the wall below. Here you rejoin the Coast Path. (For **Walk B** resume text at point 4 for the seaward return.)

3 Just beyond the gate turn LEFT down a faint green track, through a gate and on past a sewerage works to a kissing gate giving access to Mynydd Penarfynydd. Angle LEFT to follow a path up the part gorse covered slope to a small gate and on up to a trig point – *offering extensive views from Bardsey across Cardigan Bay to the mountainous coast of Snowdonia extending south towards Pembrokeshire*. Continue along the path, shortly joining another to reach the small crag at the tip of the headland. Return to the path junction, then continue north along the path, soon rising. The path then descends to a boundary and passes just above a large farm before continuing beside a wall to a small gate and on to join your outward route at the kissing gate. Return up the track to go through the gate at point 3.

4 Now follow the delightful wide Coast Path beneath Graig Fawr and across the

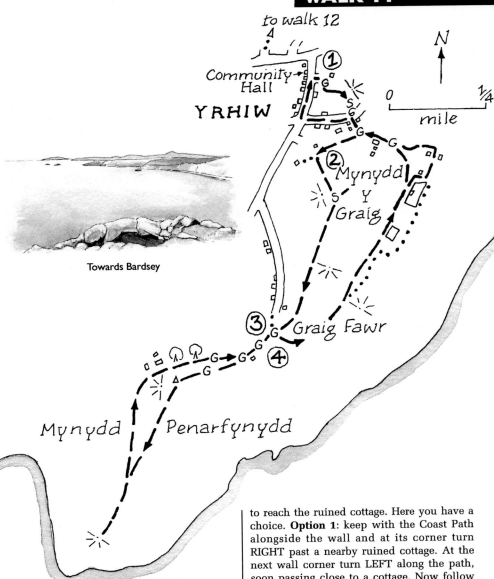

to walk 12

Community Hall

YRHIW

① G S G

② Mynydd Y Graig S G

G G

Mynydd y Graig

Towards Bardsey

N

0   ¼
mile

③ G G Graig Fawr ④
G G G
A G

Mynydd   Penarfynydd

sea-facing mid slopes of Mynydd y Graig. When it splits go up the left fork – *enjoying a panorama of mountains from the Rivals, Snowdon and down the coast to Cadair Idris and beyond.* Later the path narrows and continues towards a distant cottage ahead. The path passes above a walled enclosure to reach the ruined cottage. Here you have a choice. **Option 1**: keep with the Coast Path alongside the wall and at its corner turn RIGHT past a nearby ruined cottage. At the next wall corner turn LEFT along the path, soon passing close to a cottage. Now follow a wide green path up past another cottage to a gate. **Option 2**: follow a path on the left angling up across the slope then descending to reach a gate. Both routes then continue up the narrow green track past terraced cottages to join the outward route. At the road turn LEFT then at crossroads, turn RIGHT back to the start.

MYNYDD RHIW

DESCRIPTION A 3½ mile (**A**) or 3 mile (**B**) walk exploring an attractive upland area, once the site of a Neolithic axe factory, now an Open Access area, part owned by the National Trust. Although only 997 ft/304 metres high it offers good views and enjoyable walking on a choice of paths and green tracks. Allow about 2¼ hours.

START Mynydd Rhiw National Trust sign (off-road parking). SH 237298.

DIRECTIONS See Walk 11.

Follow the wide track up the hillside, passing a side track on the left. Keep with the main track as it heads up towards the radio relay station. *Near the track on the right (N) is the site of an important Neolithic (Stone Age) Axe factory. Shale was quarried from several shallow pits and made into polished narrow axes, which have been found far away from here.* When it levels out head half-RIGHT on a narrow green track to pass the compound with its mast. Continue to the trig point ahead for all-round views, then follow a path along its small ridge. The path soon bends LEFT through heather to join the main ridge track. Follow it south towards another hilltop transmitter mast. After passing between walls, as it starts to descend, take a green track angling RIGHT. At another green track at a good viewpoint, do a u-turn and follow it to the end of a road. The nearby access track leads up the nearby mast compound, from where the top of the distinctive small hill is accessible.

2 From an informal parking area near the road end follow a waymarked path south east to a stone stile. Follow the path ahead, soon bending down to the boundary wall corner of a house. Now follow a green track up past a telegraph pole. When it splits by

small crags you have a choice. (For **Walk B** take the right fork and follow the track to a ladder-stile and on to reach the road by a house. Follow the road back to the start.)

3 For **Walk A** continue with the green track past waymarked side paths. Shortly leave the track and head to cross a stone stile in the wall on your left. Follow a path through low gorse, then after about 20 yards turn RIGHT along anoth-

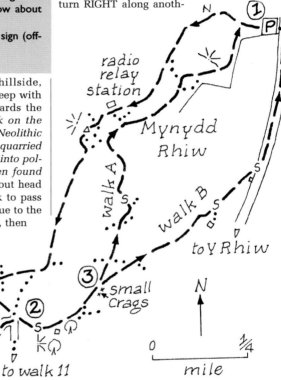

er path up towards the mast, later bending up towards the trig point to join the main ridge track. Follow it RIGHT. At a crossroad of tracks, take the one on the right. Shortly, divert to a small top with a low stone shelter. Follow a path ahead, crossing a narrow green track, to reach another rocky top. Return to the track just crossed and turn LEFT to rejoin your earlier track which steadily descends to join your outward route.

WALK 13
MYNYDD MAWR TO MYNYDD BYCHESTYN

DESCRIPTION An exhilarating 4 mile walk linking two Open Access headlands, featuring dramatic cliff-top scenery and great views and a recommended café to finish. Please take care for the cliff slopes are steep in places. Allow about 2½ hours.
START Braich-y-Pwll, Uwchmynydd. SH 142256.
DIRECTIONS See Walk 15.

rejoin the Coast Path. From its corner follow the path back towards the sea, soon rising across the steep craggy slope then bending south east past a waymark post and bending inland to another. (Here you can continue on the Coast Path up beneath the eastern slopes of Mynydd Gwyddel. As it begins to level out angle right to the hidden waymark post at point 3.) Descend and follow a path up onto the next rocky headland, climb to its highest point, then head inland across its rocky top, and down to a Coast Path waymark post at point 3.

3 Descend to a small gate below. Continue along the cliff-top Coast Path to another small gate, then a kissing gate. When it splits take the left fork. When the path bends left keep ahead up to a waymark post on the skyline. The Coast Path rises steadily across Mynydd Bychestyn to join a fence overlooking Parwyd inlet, with its massive 300 ft cliff face ahead. At the fence corner turn LEFT along the wide path to a kissing gate by a National Trust Bychestyn sign.

4 Ignore the kissing gate, but continue along a narrow green track beside the boundary, through a gate and on to a lane. Follow it RIGHT and on the bend turn LEFT to follow a signposted path along a track. Go through a facing gate, cross a stile ahead, then go half-RIGHT across the field to a stile/gate. Head LEFT to a waymarked gate near a large shed and follow the access track to the road. Follow it LEFT to Mynydd café for home-made refreshments then back to the start.

Information Centre
P
Mynydd Mawr — seat
P (1)
café
(2)
Mynydd Gwyddel
St Mary's Well
(3)
N
0   ¼
mile
G
G
G
S-G
S-G
G
walk 14
G
(4) to Pen y Cil
Mynydd Bychestyn
Parwyd

1 Go up the road, and just after it bends, head towards a seat above a small crag. Rejoin the single track road just beyond and follow it up to its end at the summit beneath the information centre. Now follow the instructions in paragraph 2 (choosing **route A**) and paragraph 3 of **Walk 15**.

2 Continue up beside the stream, cross it to reach the small fenced area above to

WALK 14

PORTH MEUDWY & PEN Y CIL

DESCRIPTION A 6 mile (**A**) or 5½ mile (**B**) walk along a the cliff-top Coast Path via Porth Meudwy to the attractive headland of Pen y Cil owned by the National Trust, returning by a choice of routes. The route includes shorter 3 mile (**C**) or 2¾ mile (**D**) walks. At Aberdaron there is a choice of cliff-top path or the beach, which allows you to vary the outward and return sections according to the tide. Allow about 3½ hours.

START Aberdaron. SH 172264.

DIRECTIONS Aberdaron lies at the end of the B4413, where there is a large car park (*note closing times*) near the new Visitor Centre.

*A*berdaron, *an old fishing village at the mouth of the river Daron, has historically been a place of embarkation for people on pilgrimage to the celebrated monastery on Bardsey. In the early 19thC the village was isolated because of poor roads and relied on sea transport, with market days in Pwllheli in summer providing most of their needs. Boats also sailed weekly to Liverpool with pigs, poultry & eggs, returning with coal.*

St Hywyn's church, dating from the 12thC, is dedicated to Hywyn, a Bretton Saint and an Abbot on Bardsey Island, who established a wooden church here in the 5thC. After part of the churchyard was lost to the sea, the church was abandoned and a new church built high above the village. However it was found wanting and this delightful old church was subsequently restored. An available leaflet tells you more about its history and interesting features, including two early 6thC Christian Stones. The church still receives thousands of visitors a year.

Aberdaron had a monastic community linked to that on Bardsey. In medieval times the monastery on Bardsey had many lands and privileges on the mainland. A court and exchequer was established at Cwrt, giving the farm its name, where the legal and administrative duties were conducted, and hangings took place nearby.

1 Cross the 17thC stone bridge and follow the road past 13thC Y Gegin Fawr – *reputedly the last eating place for pilgrims before the crossing to Bardsey* – round to visit St. Hywyn's church. Return to the bend. You now have a choice of options to point 2

For the beach option go between Eleri stores and cottages to reach the promenade. Follow it to its end, then go along the beach, soon crossing the Afon Daron. At the far end of the rock slab sea defence cross a stream beneath the cliff. Go through a kissing gate and up the stepped path via another kissing gate on to the cliffs.

For the cliff-top option, cross the stone bridge over the river, then just past Henfaes turn LEFT on a road signposted to Porth Oer. Follow it up the hill past a side road. Just beyond the speed deristriction sign go through a small metal gate above a kissing gate, on the left into National Trust owned Porth Simdde land. Follow the recently created fenced section of Coast Path along the cliffs, then down stone steps to a large footbridge over the stream to join the beach route at a kissing gate. Go up the stepped path to a kissing gate and on to the cliffs.

2 Follow the Coast Path south along the cliffs later passing through kissing gates and descending to Porth Meudwy (Hermit Cove) – *the traditional landing place for boats from Bardsey Island, and still used by lobster and crab fishermen.* (For **Walk D**, turn right and follow the track up the valley to the road, which you follow back to Aberdaron.) The Coast path now crosses a footbridge, rises to a kissing gate and continues along the cliffs. Later the path bends up and passes beneath a small crag above Porth Cloch, then rises inland past a waymark post to another one just before a kissing gate. (For **Walk C**, go through the kissing gate, then follow the fence on the right and through a gateway in it. Follow the waymarked path along the right-hand edge of a long field, through a gateway in the corner and on through a gate ahead to go down a narrow hedge-lined path to the road. Follow it right to rejoin the main route back to Aberdaron.)

3 Continue with the cliff-top Coast Path passing through two kissing gates above the old quay at Porth y Pistyll – *built in the early 20thC to ship locally quarried stone.* Later it curves round above Hen Borth to another kissing gate. Continue with the path to a further kissing gate near the end of Pen y Cil headland – *which is home to a colony of choughs.* Angle RIGHT up the Coast Path, past a waymark post, then a good view across to nearby Bardsey, and on up to reach a small stone cairn at the top of Pen y Cil – *offering extensive all-round views. Nearby is the 300ft compressed cliff face of Parwyd.* The path continues northwards to a kissing gate. (For **Walk B** continue ahead down the field and through a gate by a cottage. Follow its access track to join a road. Follow it to join Walk A at point 5.)

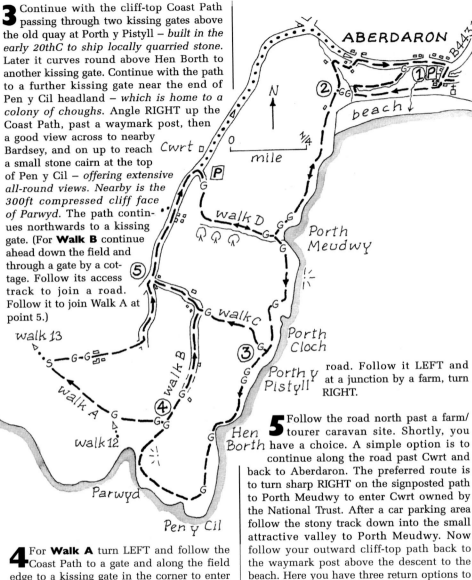

4 For **Walk A** turn LEFT and follow the Coast Path to a gate and along the field edge to a kissing gate in the corner to enter Bychestyn owned by the National Trust. Continue ahead along the narrow green track near the boundary, then just before a gate cross a ladder-stile on the right. Follow the gated path through the edge of two fields, go along a track to pass between farm buildings, then follow its access track to the road. Follow it LEFT and at a junction by a farm, turn RIGHT.

5 Follow the road north past a farm/tourer caravan site. Shortly, you have a choice. A simple option is to continue along the road past Cwrt and back to Aberdaron. The preferred route is to turn sharp RIGHT on the signposted path to Porth Meudwy to enter Cwrt owned by the National Trust. After a car parking area follow the stony track down into the small attractive valley to Porth Meudwy. Now follow your outward cliff-top path back to the waymark post above the descent to the beach. Here you have three return options to Aberdaron: by beach, by continuing with the Coast Path down and back up onto the cliffs to the road, or the following described route. Continue ahead with the path to a footbridge onto a track by cottages. Follow it up to join the road, soon descending and enjoying good views of this ancient community.

MYNYDD MAWR & MYNYDD GWYDDEL

DESCRIPTION A 2¼ mile (**A**) or simpler 1¾ mile (**B**) walk exploring the attractive headland, part owned by the National Trust, and now Open Access land, at the end of the Llŷn Peninsula overlooking Bardsey island. The route climbs to the summit of Mynydd Mawr, either by an ancient well and a nearby top for good views, then up a new section of the Coast Path (Walk A) or simply by following the meandering single track road (Walk B). After visiting the former coastguard hut the route descends towards Bardsey. Walk A follows the Coast Path across the steeper seaward edges, then descends to the narrow rocky inlet from where traditionally pilgrims sailed across to Bardsey Island, and where you can see St Mary's Well at low tide. Walk B makes a more inland approach. The route then climbs to the top of Mynydd Gwyddel for new views. Please take care for the slopes are steep in places. Allow about 1½ – 2 hours.

START Braich-y-Pwll, Uwchmynydd. SH 142256.

DIRECTIONS About 1 mile before Aberdaron, turn off the B4413 at a small hamlet, on a road signposted to Uwchmynydd. Follow the road through the scattered settlement of Uwchmynydd, past Mynydd cafe to enter National Trust Braich-y-Pwll after 2½ miles. Follow the lane to a grass parking area opposite an information board.

*F*or centuries, *nearby Bardsey Island (Ynys Enlli), where St Mary's Abbey was established in the 13thC, has provided sanctuary for religious refugees, bards and pilgrims, many of whom chose to end their days there. Such was the religious importance of the island that it was said that three pilgrimages to Bardsey equalled one to Rome! From an inlet here, tradition says that in the Middle Ages thousands of pilgrims sailed across the treacherous Bardsey Sound. Nearby are ruins said to be of St Mary's church, where prayers were offered for a safe journey, and a spring in the rocks below high tide level, known as St Mary's Well, reputedly used by pilgrims before their dangerous journey. Until the Dissolution of the monasteries, much of the tip of Llŷn was held by Bardsey Abbey. The island is now a National Nature Reserve run by the Bardsey Island Trust.*

Go up the road, and just after it bends, head towards a seat above a small crag. Rejoin the single track road just beyond. About 10 yards after a passing place, go down a green track on the right. (For **Walk B** continue up the road.) Go past an old walled enclosure. Nearby is the site of Ffynnon Cerydd well. Keep ahead up the green track, soon levelling out – *with good views towards Aberdaron, the distant mountains of Snowdonia, and the Cambrian Coast.* Just before it begins to gently descend take a path on the left up to the nearby rocky top for new views northwards to Porth Llanllawen and Mynydd Carreg. Now follow a sketchy path north west down across the low gorse/heather terrain towards the sea past rocks on your right to soon reach the Coast Path. Follow it LEFT steadily descending then rising, initially steeply, up the north eastern slopes of Mynydd Mawr and along its seaward side to join the road at its end.

2 After visiting the former summit coastguard hut – *an important lookout station in the World War II, with many military staff based here, and now an information centre* – follow a concrete path from the road end heading south towards Bardsey Island, later descending steps to a shelf containing the concrete foundations of several buildings. For **Walk B**, a few yards below the main foundation, bear LEFT on a path which you follow across the slope past side paths, soon descending and bending left. Head down the expansive grassy slope towards Bardsey Island aiming for the left of two crags overlooking the sea to join Walk A at point 3.

For **Walk A** descend to another green shelf below by a wide cleft in the ground. Descend to a further narrow green shelf 15 yards below, then follow the waymarked Coast Path down to a cross-path – *with good views of the swirling currents below.* Turn LEFT and follow the Coast Path above a dramatic steep slope above the sea. When the Coast Path starts bending left take a fainter path angling ahead down the slope, then continue down the edge of the expansive grassy headland to pass a small crag to reach another lower down overlooking the sea.

3 Now head across open ground towards a distant small fenced enclosure on the lower slopes of Mynydd Gwyddel. At the lower end of a small hollow just before reaching a stream, a path leads down to the sea above the western edge of the narrow rocky cove from where pilgrims reputedly sailed to Bardsey. A short scramble with care down the rock band brings you to just above the sea. To the right in the rock face is a tiny pool with water trickling down from a freshwater spring to the sea – *St Mary's Well.* Retrace your steps.

4 Cross the stream and continue up alongside it. Go past the small fenced enclosure, then just before another enclosure, do a sharp u-turn to follow a wide path angling across the slopes of Mynydd Gwyddel. At its end climb up more steeply to the summit to enjoy good views along the Llŷn to the Rivals and distant Snowdonia. Follow the wide path down to the boundary corner. Go up a choice of paths ahead, then head back to the start. A visit to nearby Mynydd café is recommended.

Bardsey Island

MYNYDD CARREG TO PORTH LLANLLAWEN

DESCRIPTION A 6½ mile (**A**) exploring an attractive section of the coast near the end of the Llŷn, linking varied National Trust land. The route first visits a former lookout tower on the small hill of Mynydd Carreg, before following the delightful Coast Path to Mynydd Anelog. After crossing its western slope the route continues with the Coast Path to pass above the rocky inlet of Porth Llanllawen. The return route includes a short climb (optional) to the top of Mynydd Anelog (629 feet/192 metres) for great all-round views. Allow about 4 hours. The route includes shorter 5½ mile (**B**), or 4¼ mile (**C**) walks.
START National Trust Carreg car park. SH 162290.
DIRECTIONS Near Pen-y-groeslon, 3½ miles from Aberdaron, turn off the B4413 on a road signposted to Porth Oer/Whistling Sands. After 2 miles, at a split turning on the right, keep ahead signposted to Aberdaron/Uwchmynydd, shortly passing the turning to Whistling Sands. Continue along the road past woodland. Just beyond Carreg Plas/ farm and bungalows the NT car park is signposted up a narrow stony track on the right.

The information board reveals that Carreg (stone) takes its name from jasper, a semi-precious stone found locally and mined in the 18th and 19thC for decorative designs. The property was owned by the Carreg family from the 14thC until the mid-20thC.

Go through the kissing gate, then bear RIGHT up to another kissing gate and on up to the small tower for good views of Whistling Sands. Return to the kissing gate then go half-RIGHT down the large field to join a kissing gated enclosed path to reach the Coast Path. Follow it LEFT as it meanders along the cliffs. After ⅓ mile, the path bends and descends into a small side valley. Just before a small sleeper bridge and a ladder-stile beyond, do a sharp U-turn RIGHT down to a gated footbridge. Continue with the Coast Path to a small gate. The wide path now rises steadily to another small gate. Continue with the main path up the heather/ bracken covered hillside, later descending to a green track in a small depression. Continue up to join a another green track coming in from the left.

2 Shortly, when it splits just before a small fenced enclosure, go up the right fork, shortly levelling out – *with a view ahead of Mynydd Anelog.* Here divert to the right to a headland giving good views south to Mynydd Mawr, then return to the track and follow it past a side track at point 6 – your return route or **Walk C** option. The delightful track rises gently, then continues past a fence-topped wall, with a cottage nearby. At its next corner follow a path angling away to a nearby waymark post. The delightful wide Coast Path continues across the steep western slopes of Mynydd Anelog. At a waymark post the path bends inland and descends steadily to another post. (For **Walk B** follow a path ahead near the boundary beneath Mynydd Anelog to join the return route at point 5.)

3 For **Walk A** do a sharp U-turn RIGHT and follow the Coast Path beside the boundary to its corner, then down to a small gate. The Coast Path now descends to a waymark post and continues down through bracken, past another post and on by the fence to a viewpoint overlooking Porth Llanllawen. The path now bends LEFT and continues just below the fence, then angles away to cross a stream. Follow the path rising LEFT, soon zig zagging, before continuing below a fence. It then makes a long steady descent to cross a footbridge below a National Trust sign. Turn LEFT, taking the lower left fork, soon bending up to a waymark post overlooking an inlet. Here you leave the Coast Path, which continues up to Mynydd Mawr, by turning LEFT on a narrow path along the top edge of the side valley. After a few yards join a higher path just above and continue below the fence. Just before a waymark post in the fence corner, turn LEFT down to cross the stream and up to a stile by an old telegraph pole. Keep ahead, initially beside the boundary, then across the field to a fence corner ahead. Continue beside the fence. At a gate in the corner, bear LEFT to the other corner and continue between fences to gates, and on to a nearby farm track. Follow it RIGHT up to join a stony track.

4 Go up the stony track, passing above a cottage. Just before the former farm of Bryn Sander go through a kissing gate on the left and up the field edge past an out-

building to a kissing gate. Go across the next field to a stile, then follow the boundary on the left to cross a nearby cottage's access track. Continue beside the boundary on the left up to a small gate back into National Trust and Open Access land, where you are joined by Walk B.

5 Continue up the path ahead by the boundary. At a post, take the left fork to pass behind a cottage. From behind the cottage, a short steep climb takes you to the top of Mynydd Anelog for extensive views. (Alternatively continue on the wide green path across its lower slopes.) Continue along the ridge to a small cairn, then follow a descending path towards the sea, soon taking another path down to join the lower path just above a cottage. Follow it down to join your outward route at the wall corner. Continue along the green track.

6 Shortly on the bend, turn RIGHT down another green track, soon bending left beside the boundary – *offering good views east* – and continuing past the small enclosure to rejoin your outward route again. Follow it down to the track junction. Continue down its right fork past a cottage to a gate. At a farm go through a gate at the end of a stone barn on the right. Follow the waymarked path along the field edge and through a gate. Keep ahead, go through a small gate and along a short path to the road. Follow it LEFT to a junction and back to the start.

Mynydd Carreg — walk 17

N

0   ¼ mile

Mynydd Anelog
walk B
Porth Llanllawen

PORTH OER

DESCRIPTION An extended 3 mile figure of eight walk featuring the popular Porth Oer (also known as Whistling Sands, reputedly due to its white sand 'whistling' as you walk on it), and the adjoining coastline owned by the National Trust. The route follows the cliff-top Coast Path above the beach, explores the delightful cliffs above Porth y Wrach, then returns along the beautiful beach to a cafe and up the road to the car park. It then follows the cliff-top Coast Path south-west, before heading inland to pass beneath Mynydd Carreg with its former lookout tower, then returning by road. Allow about 2 hours. It can easily be undertaken as two separate short walks.

START Whistling Sands car park. SH 166295.

DIRECTIONS Near Pen-y-groeslon, 3½ miles north east of Aberdaron, turn off the B4413 on a road signposted to Porth Oer/Whistling Sands. After 2 miles, at a split turning on the right, keep ahead signposted to Aberdaron/Uwchmynydd, shortly reaching the turning to Whistling Sands.

1 Leave the car park from the bottom right-hand corner by an information board. Cross the road and follow the signposted Coast Path opposite between hedges, then along the cliffs overlooking the beach at Porth Oer to a kissing gate. Continue with the path, later descending to another kissing gate. Turn RIGHT and follow the path to the higher of two kissing gates accessing another area of headland owned by the National Trust. Walk along the cliff edge to Porth y Wrach then retrace your steps to follow a path onto the beach. Walk along it to the café/shop at the road end. After refreshments go up the road to re-enter the car park.

2 Follow the signposted Coast Path between toilets and through trees, then towards the sea to a kissing gate on the cliffs. Follow the Coast Path along the cliffs, later bending inland towards the former hilltop lookout tower. Just after it bends right cross stiles on the left. Go up the edge of the large field to a gate in the corner. Follow a green track LEFT up to gates and on to the road. Follow it LEFT to the turning for the car park.

Porth y Wrâch

Porth Oer

N

0   ½   mile

② ① P

S S

G   G

tower
o
Mynydd
Carreg

WALK 18
PORTH COLMON

DESCRIPTION A 3¾ mile walk following the cliff-top Coast Path from Traeth Penllech to Porth Colmon and on to Porth Ty-mawr, returning by minor roads. Allow about 2½ hours.
START Pont yr Afon Fawr car park, near Traeth Penllech. SH 206341.
DIRECTIONS See Walk 19.

1 From the entrance turn LEFT then take a nearby signposted path to a viewpoint overlooking Traeth Penllech and down to the beach. Turn LEFT, cross the Afon Fawr, then take a stepped path up to a gate and on to the top of the cliffs. Continue along the cliff-top Coast Path, shortly being joined by another path from the beach. Later the path gradually descends to a gate by a small building at a stony track It then rises back onto the cliffs

and continues down to a road end at Porth Colmon. Go through a car parking area by a house, then follow the signposted Coast Path over a footbridge by the rocky shore and back onto the low cliffs to a kissing gate. Continue with the cliff-top path beside the fence past Porth Wen Bach to a kissing gate. The path continues along the cliffs to a finger post at an old boundary corner overlooking Porth Ty-mawr. Below is a footbridge and kissing gate.

2 Here you leave the Coast Path by heading inland alongside the old boundary past a post and briefly on the embanked boundary by the fence. The path continues below the old boundary near a stream to a small gate. Turn LEFT along the field edge to a waymark post. Head RIGHT across the field, through a waymarked wide gap in the boundary, and along the narrow field to a kissing gate. Continue round the field edge above an old reedy sunken track. Just before a small ruined cottage, turn LEFT to a nearby waymarked gate. Continue along the enclosed green track to join an access track from a nearby house. At a minor road follow it LEFT to a junction at the hamlet of Pen-y-graig. Turn RIGHT and at crossroads LEFT again. Follow the quiet country road back to the start.

25

TRAETH PENLLECH & PORTH YCHAIN

DESCRIPTION A 4 mile walk along the cliff-top Coast Path from the long sandy beach of Traeth Penllech to the small cove of Porth Ychain, returning by quiet country road. Avoid at high tide when the first 200 yards along the beach will be inaccessible. Allow about 2 hours. Combining the beach and cliff-top path makes an alternative 1½ mile walk by Traeth Penllech.
START Pont yr Afon Fawr car park, near Traeth Penllech. SH 206341.
DIRECTIONS Travelling south from Tudweiliog on the B4417, after 1¾ miles and a bend/ junction take a minor road on the right. At a junction, turn left for ¾ mile to the car park.

Turn briefly along the road and take the signposted gated path to cliffs overlooking Traeth Penllech and down to the beach. Walk along its edge for about 200 yards, then after crossing a stream head to a stile/gate (or join the cliff-top path further along the beach) and climb on to the cliffs. After a gate, the Coast Path rises right and goes along the higher cliffs, later descending to just above the beach. It then continues along the cliffs to eventually reach Porth Ychain. Descend to the small stony cove. Head to a waymark post above a stream at the far side. Go up the wide path, past another waymark post to follow the path ahead inland through gorse to a gate. Go along the narrow path to a cottage. Follow the lane ahead past another cottage, then Tyddyn Belyn farm to the road, which you follow back to the start.

PORTH YSGADEN & PORTH YCHAIN

DESCRIPTION A 3 mile walk (**A**) from Porth Ysgaden – *once a haven for herring boats and now used by local fishermen and sub-aqua divers* – along the cliffs to the small cove of Porth Ychain, returning by quiet country road. Allow about 1½ hours. An alternative 1¾ mile (**B**) walk to Porth Gwylan is included.
START Porth Ysgaden car park. SH 220374.
DIRECTIONS See Walk 21.

Go through a kissing gate near the boat compound and follow the Coast Path along the low cliffs. After a kissing gate, the path passes above Porth Gwylan, accessible by steps, to reach a finger post. (For **Walk B** go through the kissing gate and along the green track to pass through a farm, then follow its access track to a minor road. Turn LEFT, then take a side road on the left past a farm and on to meet the track leading to Porth Ysgaden.)

For **Walk A** continue along the cliffs, later passing through two kissing gates in quick succession, before bending briefly inland. After another kissing gate the path continues along the cliffs, shortly meeting another path at a waymark post just before Porth Ychain. Descend to the small stony cove, then return to the waymark post. Now follow the other path inland through gorse to a gate and on to a cottage. Follow the lane ahead past another cottage, then Tyddyn Belyn farm to the road. Follow it LEFT back to the track leading to Porth Ysgaden.

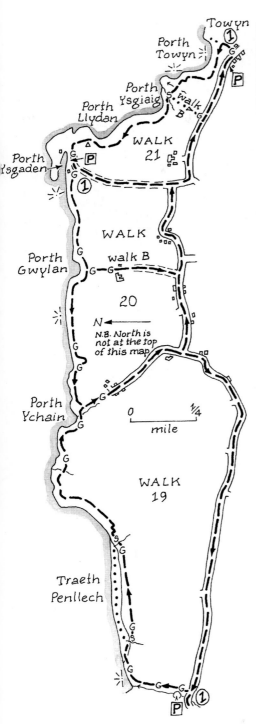

WALK 21

PORTH TOWYN & PORTH YSGADEN

DESCRIPTION A 2¼ mile walk (**A**) along the rocky coast from Porth Towyn, with its popular sandy beach, to the small natural harbour at Porth Ysgaden, returning by quiet country roads. Allow about 1½ hours. The route includes a 1 mile walk to Porth Ysglaig (**B**).

START Car park, Porth Towyn SH 232374 or Porth Ysgaden car park. SH 220374.

DIRECTIONS As you enter Tudweiliog from Nefyn on the B4417, take a minor road signposted to the beach for almost 1 mile to reach Towyn farm. At the end of outbuildings is a parking area kindly provided by the farmer. Alternatively, continue along the road, turn right at the junction, then on the next bend, keep ahead along a stony track signposted to Porth Ysgaden.

Go through a gate opposite the farm's entrance on the path signposted to Traeth Towyn. Soon, bear LEFT along the cliffs overlooking Porth Towyn's sandy beach. At the end of caravans go through an old embanked boundary and follow a path across a small field, soon bending RIGHT along the cliffs by another old boundary. Shortly descend to a hidden stile and footbridge at Porth Ysglaig. Cross a small caravan site to its access track. (For **Walk B** follow it to the road.) At the finger post beyond, go up the wide path signposted to Porth Ysgaden and continue along the cliffs above the rocky coastline and clear sea, later passing a trig point, then near an old embanked boundary. *In a small cove below are several boats and sheds.* At a waymark post turn LEFT beside the embankment to a kissing gate into the car park at Porth Ysgaden – *with a gable end ruin nearby.* Follow the access track to a minor road. Keep ahead, then at the junction turn LEFT back to the start.

MORFA NEFYN TO PORTH TOWYN

DESCRIPTION A delightful 8 mile linear walk via Porth Dinllaen (see Walk 23 for information) following the cliff-top Coast Path along a splendid section of the rocky coastline linking two popular sandy bays, with seabirds and occasional seals swimming in the clear turquoise sea for company. With options for circular walks limited and a regular bus service available – no. 8 Pwllheli bus from Tudweiliog (visit www.gwynedd.gov.uk or www.traveline.info for details), this is the best way of enjoying this sec-

tion of unspoilt coast. Allow about 5 hours.
START Tudweiliog SH 238368 or car park at Towyn farm, Porth Towyn. SH 232374.
Walk start: Lon Golff, Morfa Nefyn. SH 283405.
DIRECTIONS Tudweiliog lies on the B4417 south west of Morfa Nefyn. Towyn farm is reached by minor road from the B4417. At the end of outbuildings is a parking area kindly provided by the farmer (small fee).

1 Catch the no. 8 Pwllheli bus from the village stores. At Morfa Nefyn it turns off the B4417 along Lon Las, and at cross-roads turns right. Alight at a bus stop about 70 yards from the cross-roads (Rhos Bridin).

2 From the crossroads, go along Lon Golff to the golf club, then follow the lane down the golf course to a waymarked path junction just beyond a large building. (If you wish to leave Porth Dinllaen for another time turn left along the golf course, past a small circular fenced area, then up to another waymark post by tee 10. Turn right down across the golf course to a way-

mark post overlooking Borth Wen at point 3.) Continue along the stony track, soon forking down to Porth Dinllaen. If high tide return to the track and continue along the cliff-top to the lifeboat station. Otherwise go past the Ty Coch inn and cottages to follow a path round the headland above the rocky shore past a cottage and on to the lifeboat station. From the top of its access track, go past the nearby

mast and follow a path round the headland above the rocky shoreline, then climb up to pass to the left of a former lookout tower. Follow the Coast Path along the western edge of the golf course overlooking the rocky coast, later bending above the shingly beach of Borth Wen.

28

3 Continue with the waymarked Coast Path along the edge of the golf course, later bending above Aber Geirch to a kissing gate and descending to cross a footbridge over a river. The path now bears RIGHT, briefly near the river, climbs the slope ahead, passes in front of a small rock face then bends up to a kissing gate. The gated Coast Path continues along the cliffs, later descending to a finger post to cross a stream at a shingly cove, then rises to a kissing gate. It continues along the cliffs to a small gate by a finger

4 Shortly the path descends via two more kissing gates to a small shingly cove, crosses a stream and rises back onto the cliffs. Distant caravans indicate your destination. After the next kissing gate look ahead to see a small Natural Arch. Continue along the gated Coast Path to eventually reach a finger post by an access path leading down to the beach at Porth Towyn. Nearby seats offer a good view overlooking the small bay. Head inland past caravans to the road by Towyn farm. Go through the farmyard and along a wide hedge-lined track to a gate. Follow a green track up the field edge to gates, then go up the edge of the next field to a kissing gate at a caravan site entrance. Follow its access track up to the main road in Tudweiliog.

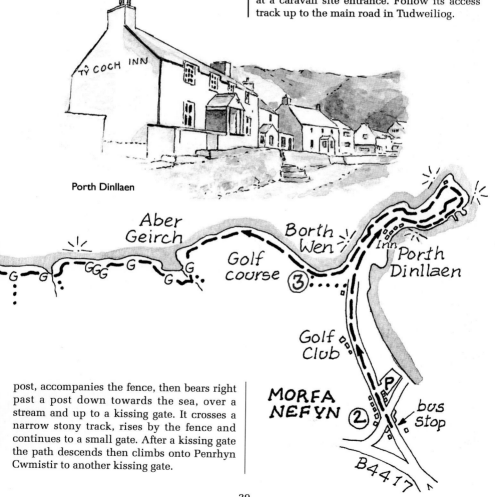

Porth Dinllaen

post, accompanies the fence, then bears right past a post down towards the sea, over a stream and up to a kissing gate. It crosses a narrow stony track, rises by the fence and continues to a small gate. After a kissing gate the path descends then climbs onto Penrhyn Cwmistir to another kissing gate.

WALK 23

PORTH DINLLAEN

DESCRIPTION A 3 mile walk, combining beach (at low tide) and cliff-top walking around a delightful narrow headland, featuring the old fishing hamlet of Port Dinllaen nestling beneath the cliffs, with its shoreline 19thC inn and wonderful coastal views. An alternative high tide route is included. Allow about 1½ hours.

START National Trust car park, Morfa Nefyn. SH 282407.

DIRECTIONS At crossroads in Morfa Nefyn, turn off the B4417 along Lon Pen Rhos. At minor crossroads, continue ahead along Lon Golff to the car park on the right.

The *long narrow headland protects the only good natural harbour on the northern coast of Llŷn, which was once a busy port, with over 600 vessels visiting a year by the end of the 18thC. During the early 19thC, there were serious proposals for it to be developed as the main port for Ireland, with a railway link to Bangor, but eventually Holyhead was chosen instead. The Ty Coch, built in 1823 as a vicarage, became an inn in 1842 to service workers in the shipbuilding yards on the beach. Overlooking Porth Dinllaen near the inn are the remains of an Iron Age coastal promontory fort.*

From the car park's far corner follow a path down to the road by toilets to reach the beach. Walk along the beach past a house, then two cottages at a small headland. Continue along the beach to Porth Dinllaen. From the Tŷ Coch inn go past cottages to the Caban Griff containing history about Porth Dinllaen. From its rear follow a path above the rocky shore past a house and continue to the lifeboat station.

High tide alternative: Follow Lon Golff up to the golf club, then the lane down the golf course to a large building. Continue with the Coast Path along the stony track, soon forking down a concrete road to Porth Dinllaen. From the Ty Coch inn return to continue along the cliff-top track.

2 From the flagpole at the top of the lifeboat station's access track follow a path above the shore round to a seat and on above the rocky shoreline, then climb up to pass to the left of a former lookout tower. Follow the Coast Path along the low cliffs overlooking the rocky coast at the western edge of the golf course, guided by occasional waymark posts, passing a large fenced depression, then later bending above the shingly beach of Borth Wen. At a waymarked path junction turn LEFT across the golf course to another waymark post. Turn LEFT towards the large building then follow the lane up to the golf club. Go down the road to the car park.

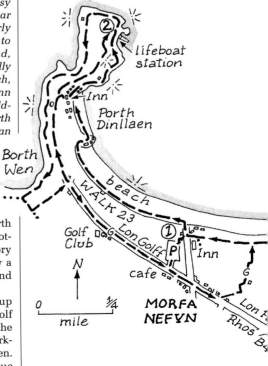

30

WALK 24

PENRHYN NEFYN

DESCRIPTION A 3¾ mile walk, following the cliff-top Coast Path from Nefyn via the headland of Penrhyn Nefyn to Morfa Nefyn (pub and cafe refreshment options), returning partly by a delightful enclosed path and quiet road. Allow about 2 hours. At low tide the beach offers an alternative start or a simple 1¼ mile walk combined with the cliff-top path.

START Beach car park, Nefyn SH 302407 or a car park on the B4417 SH 303405.

DIRECTIONS From the crossroads in Nefyn, head west on the B4417 (Aberdaron). Shortly, take the road signposted to the beach, or continue to the alternative car park/amenity centre by the police station.

Nefn has an interesting history. St Mary's church was founded in the 6thC and for centuries served pilgrims on route to Bardsey. In the 11thC a motte and bailey castle was built here, indicating the area's strategic importance. In 1284, Edward 1 held a tournament in Nefyn to celebrate his conquest over the Welsh, and in 1355 it was granted Royal Borough status. Its natural harbour allowed it to develop as an important commercial centre. It was renowned for its herring fishing, which flourished until the end of World War I, reflected in the three herrings in its coat of arms. The town was sometimes referred to as 'Nefyn the fish' and the herrings as 'Nefyn beef'. In the 18th and 19thC, shipbuilding at Nefyn and Porth Dinllaen became important, with boatyards on the seashore producing small wooden sailing vessels. Former 19thC St Mary's church is now a Heritage Centre/Maritime Museum.

1 From the beach car park return up the road. (Or at low tide walk along the beach to the hamlet and small harbour beneath Penrhyn Nefyn, then from the slipway beneath the first building, take a path up to join the Coast Path.) At the top follow the signposted raised Coast Path past a near-by castellated house and along the cliffs past seats, later passing the descent path to the beach. Turn RIGHT briefly along a narrow lane. On the bend follow the Coast Path along the eastern side of Porth Nefyn headland to its tip. Return a few yards, then follow a path back along its western side, before continuing along the cliffs.

2 Shortly, the path bends inland to a house and follows its access track to a minor road. Follow it RIGHT. On the bend go along a narrow access track ahead, then a hedge-lined path. Continue along the cliff-top path, past two side paths and one later leading to the Cliffs Inn, to descend to a road. Go up the stepped path opposite from toilets, then through the large NT car park to Lon Golff and a café. Turn LEFT to crossroads and go along Lon Pen Rhos. Shortly, take a signposted path on the left between houses and along a delightful meandering hedge-lined green track to Waen cottage. Continue along a narrow hedge-lined path to a kissing gate and on to rejoin the Coast Path. Follow it back to the minor road, then continue along it to the B4417. Follow it into Nefyn.

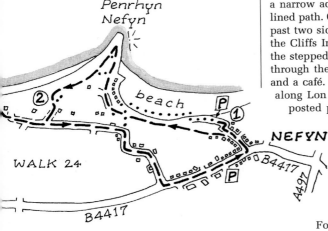

Penrhyn Nefyn

beach

NEFYN

WALK 24

B4417

B4417

A497

MOEL TY-GWYN

DESCRIPTION A 5 mile walk of varied interest and views, across a coastal landscape containing small hills quarried for granite. The route first visits Nefyn watchtower, then follows the Coast Path, passing beneath Gwylwyr Carreglefain, to ancient St Beuno's Church at Pistyll, before returning inland via Moel Ty-gwyn and Coed Mynydd. Allow about 4 hours.

START Car park, Stryd y Plas, Nefn. SH 309404 or Pistyll National Trust car park. SH 330422.

DIRECTIONS Entering Nefyn on the B4417 from the east, at crossroads by a mini-roundabout where it meets the A497 take the road angling left (Y Groes) to find the large car park on the left by the former Seion B chapel (1904). It is also signposted from the A497 in Nefyn. See Walk 26 for the Pistyll start.

From the car park entrance turn RIGHT along the road to the crossroads/mini-roundabout. Cross to the shop then go along the right-hand side of Pen-y Bryn (the B4417 to Aberdaron). Soon turn RIGHT to visit the signposted watchtower by toilets. *The watchtower is a rare small maritime tower used as a sailors' lookout during the heyday of herring fishing and shipbuilding. It was built about 1846 to replace a timber tower sited on the mound of a former 11thC motte and bailey castle.* Return to the crossroads and turn LEFT along Strydy y Ffynnon past St. Mary's Well. Continue along the road, then just before the bend go through an alleyway on the right to Stryd y Llan. Follow it LEFT past the entrance to the former 19thC St Mary's church — *now a Heritage Centre depicting the area's rich maritime past.* On the bend follow the signposted enclosed Coast Path to a kissing gate, then LEFT along the field edge. At the first boundary corner it crosses a stream and continues beside another. It then bends away, soon rising, and continues up an access track. At a gate, go through an adjoining kissing gate and follow the path up beside a wall, then past Ffynnon John Morgan to a kissing gate. Continue up

the path past a cottage — *with a good view back over Nefyn to Porth Dinllaen* — and along it's green access track past other cottages to the bend of a narrow road/track. Go up the stony track.

2 When it bends up right keep ahead along an enclosed path then cross an old incline that once served the granite quarry above on Gwylwyr Carreglefain. Follow the path across the bracken-covered lower slopes of the quarried hillside to eventually reach a kissing gate by Plas Goch. Follow the path ahead to a gated stone stile, then go half-RIGHT up to a waymark post and a small gate beyond. Follow the path up to another post. Soon afterwards keep with its right fork, passing above a farm, through trees, then descending to join the farm's access road to reach the nearby B4417. Cross the road and turn LEFT past cottages, then RIGHT on the signposted Coast Path to a small iron gate and a kissing gate beyond.

3 Follow the path along the field edge — *with a good view ahead of the Rivals* — to a stile in the corner. Go along the next field edge, then at a small waymark post turn LEFT down the field towards the sea to a waymarked fence corner. Turn RIGHT to a kissing gate by a stream. Follow a path ahead beneath the fence to a kissing gate into a field and on to another kissing gate at an access road. Go through the kissing gate opposite and cross the stile ahead. Go along the field edge, negotiating a small wettish area, to a kissing gate, then along a track past cottages to join a minor road. Follow it across the nearby bridge over a stream. Just beyond follow the Coast Path up to the entrance of ancient St Beuno's Church to visit this delightful simple church (See Walk 26 for details). Return to the road and follow it past the small National Trust car park.

4 Cross the B4417 to a kissing gate opposite. Go up the field to a waymark post beyond a narrow green cross track. Go up the next field towards a tall pole in bracken to go through a gap in the old wall by boulders. Turn RIGHT alongside the wall, then just beyond a fence pole on the left, follow a path angling LEFT up the bracken-covered slope of Moel Ty-gwyn towards a visible waymark post by a small bush. The path continues up to another post on the skyline just to the right of a small quarry waste tip. Continue up

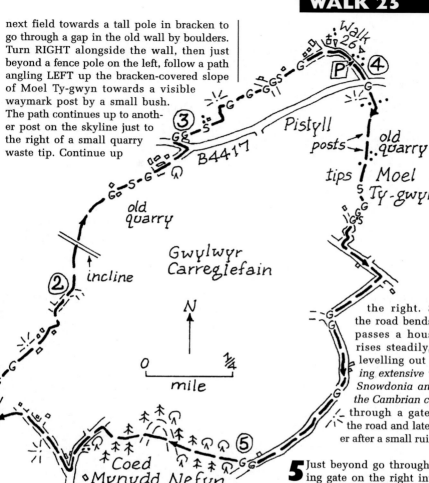

the right. Shortly the road bends south, passes a house then rises steadily, before levelling out – *offering extensive views to Snowdonia and down the Cambrian coast.* Go through a gate across the road and later another after a small ruin.

5 Just beyond go through a kissing gate on the right into Coed Mynydd Nefyn. Follow the path up through the young mixed woodland to a waymark post at a stony forestry track. Continue down a path almost opposite to rejoin the track. A few yards ahead go down a path on the right through mature conifers to a wall gap at the forest edge and on through bracken to a minor road. Follow it LEFT down past houses. When it levels out do a sharp U-turn RIGHT along a rougher access lane – *with a good view down over Nefyn.* After the entrance to Tan-y-Graig the lane descends steadily towards the sea. At the entrance to Tai Ffolt go down a narrow path between boundaries to a kissing gate onto a road. Follow it down back to the start.

the hillside and over a cross-path to join a better one just above leading from a flattish area at the top of the waste tips. Follow it RIGHT across the bracken slope to a stile in the fence ahead. *Further down are quarry waste tips and the remains of an old incline.* Follow a good path ahead to join the fence on the right overlooking the old granite quarry. Go through a waymarked gate at its end, then a small gate on the left and cross a stile just ahead by a telegraph pole. Follow the wall down to a small gate, then turn LEFT along the nearby house's access track to a minor road. Turn LEFT, then go along a road on

WALK 26

PISTYLL

DESCRIPTION A 2¾ mile walk on delightful paths exploring attractive coastal land owned by the National Trust, offering great views and the opportunity to visit a gem of an ancient church. The route first climbs across higher ground, then descends to a viewpoint over Porth y Nant, before returning with the Coast Path across a green shelf above Porth Pistyll to St. Beuno's Church. Allow about 1½ hours.
START Pistyll National Trust car park. SH 330422.
DIRECTIONS Mid-way between Llithfaen and Nefyn, turn off the B4417 at Pistyll, on a minor road signposted St Beuno's Church, to the car park.

*S*t *Beuno's* church is dedicated to the Celtic saint who founded a church here in the 6thC. This delightful simple church was an important place of worship for pilgrims on their way to Bardsey. The area later attracted many workers to quarry granite, which was shipped from a small port below Pistyll.

Go through the kissing gate and along the path, soon bending left and rising to a viewpoint overlooking the church and along the coast. After a kissing gate continue up the path near a wall, soon beneath gorse. At a kissing gate bend LEFT with the path up beside the fence-topped wall, soon bending RIGHT with the wall. From its next corner the path rises steadily, then continues near the boundary to a gate. The path continues ahead across the hillside, shortly rising again to a large boulder – *with a new view of Porth y Nant and Nant Gwytherin*. The path now descends to a small gateway and continues down to a wall. Turn LEFT, soon descending through gorse to a wide cross-path, now part of the Coast Path.

2 First follow it RIGHT down to a kissing gate overlooking Porth y Nant, then return and continue down the wide Coast Path to a gate. The path bends down

right and continues near a boundary – *with a good view towards Nefyn and Porth Dinllaen*. After a kissing gate a narrower path descends briefly then continues across the lower slope past old walls. At a tall waymark post, go to the kissing gate ahead and follow the narrow green track beside the fence to a kissing gate/gate, then down past the entrance to St Beuno's church – *well worth a visit* – to the road. Turn LEFT up the road to the start.

St Bueno's church

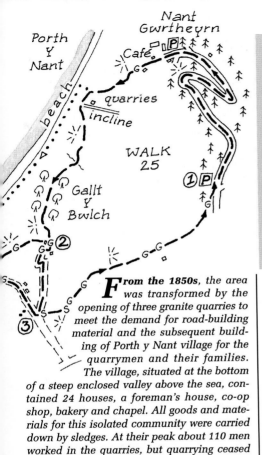

NANT GWRTHEYRN

DESCRIPTION A 3¼ mile walk featuring the dramatic setting of the former Porth y Nant quarry village, now restored as a residential Welsh Language Centre, with a Heritage Centre and cafe. The route descends by road to Nant Gwrtheyrn, then follows the Coast Path towards the shore, (offering a low tide beach option), before rising across the hillside, then after options returning across fields. Allow about 2½ hours.

START Car Park above Nant Gwrtheyrn. SH 353441. See Walk 28.

*F*rom the 1850s, the area was transformed by the opening of three granite quarries to meet the demand for road-building material and the subsequent building of Porth y Nant village for the quarrymen and their families. The village, situated at the bottom of a steep enclosed valley above the sea, contained 24 houses, a foreman's house, co-op shop, bakery and chapel. All goods and materials for this isolated community were carried down by sledges. At their peak about 110 men worked in the quarries, but quarrying ceased in the 1930s and the last family left in 1959. The village was later restored and has been used for residential Welsh courses since 1982.

Follow the road down into the forest to enter the Nant Gwrtheyrn estate. It bends sharply at a prominent viewpoint, then continues down to the former quarry village. Go down the left fork, then follow the signposted Coast Path down past the former chapel , now the Heritage Centre, to reach Caffi Meinir. Follow the surfaced path to picnic tables and a small gate below, then descend a wide path to a waymark post overlooking the beach at Porth y Nant. (For a low tide option, go along the beach to an old quarry, from where a track rises to point 3.) Turn LEFT along a path past the bottom of a former incline and old winding equipment to a finger post. Follow the Coast Path up and across the bracken covered hillside guided by occasional posts, later crossing a stream amongst trees. The path continues across Gallt y Bwlch, an area of small oak trees and an SSSI, then rises steadily.

2 Just before Ciliau-Isaf above you have a choice. (For a slightly shorter route go through a small gate above, pass above the house, then follow its access track to point 3.) Otherwise continue RIGHT along the cliff-top Coast Path, soon bending past the fence corner and passing a telegraph pole. It then bends half-LEFT to small gates and follows the field edge to a kissing gate onto an enclosed green track. Follow it LEFT up to a bungalow, then continue up its access track past a cottage to the access track from Ciliau-Isaf.

3 Cross the stile opposite and follow a path up the slope, soon alongside the old wall to an old iron ladder-stile by a small gateway. *Pause to enjoy the extensive views.* Now follow a path angling LEFT up to a small gate in the wall. At a small post just beyond turn LEFT up near an old field boundary – *with Yr Eifl ahead* – to a gate. Continue ahead up near the old boundary, then after 50 yards turn RIGHT up the slope to a post and on across the large field towards a white cottage to go through a gate in the wall corner ahead. Follow the boundary on your left through two fields (gates) then continue to the road and the start.

35

YR EIFL & TRE'R CEIRI

DESCRIPTION A 6 mile walk (**A**) that visits three of Llŷn's distinctive peaks, known as The Rivals, including Yr Eifl (1849 feet/564m), the highest mountain on the Llŷn, and Tre'r Ceiri impressive Iron Age hillfort, with excellent views throughout. Early settlers were attracted to the area by their stone, granite, iron and manganese. Allow about 4 hours. The heather and rocky terrain makes the route a demanding mountain walk for experienced walkers and should be avoided in poor visibility. The route can be shortened to a simpler 3¼ mile walk (**B**) only to Yr Eifl, with a direct return descent from its summit.

START Car Park above Nant Gwrtheyrn. SH 353441.

DIRECTIONS At the crossroads in Llithfaen, turn off the B4417 on a minor road signposted to Nant Gwrtheyrn to reach the large car park by a forest and stone sculpture.

I Return along the road to the first multi-finger post and turn sharp LEFT on the signposted bridleway/Coast Path. Follow the wide stony track across the lower western slopes of Yr Eifl – *later with views down to Nant Gwytherin* – then rising towards Bwlch yr Eifl. Near the top, follow a path alongside the wall on your left angling up towards a transmitter mast on the isolated peak. (For **Walk B** continue up the track to point 2.) Just before the wall end, turn RIGHT along a sketchy path across the stone and heather terrain, soon bearing left onto a shelf which you follow to pass between two small stone quarry buildings. Follow a path towards another building, then climb up to the mast's perimeter fence. Turn LEFT past a building to the fence corner, from where a path rises across a stony slope and up the ridge to the summit. Return down the same way then follow the access track down to rejoin the main track at Bwlch yr Eifl.

2 Opposite the access track to the transmitter mast, turn RIGHT between pylons and follow a path up Yr Eifl's heather-covered western slope. At a boulder field below the summit, the path angles LEFT guided by small cairns, then bends up to a large stone cairn with a trig point and stone windshelter on the summit. From the trig point descend the south side of the cairn. (For **Walk B**, go to another stone windshelter just ahead, then turn left down a path, soon bending right down a heather gully. The path then descends more steeply the mountain's southern slope. Later, follow the right fork down past a waymark post at a crossroad of paths and on to the start.)

For **Walk A**, turn LEFT down a path at the bottom of the stone cairn for a few yards, then take its left fork towards the hillfort of Tre'r Ceiri. Go past a sketchy side paths and continue down towards a wall in the plateau below. Soon, at a substantial crosspath above a small boulder field turn LEFT to begin a long steady descent across Yr Eifl's heather and boulder covered slope onto the heather plateau below. The path heads towards Tre'r Ceiri, fading as it passes through a short wettish reedy area, then continues towards the fort, shortly rising to an information board at it's western entrance.

3 Head up through the fort's impressive higher entrance. Turn LEFT to begin a clockwise circuit of the spectacular fort, with its massive ramparts and hut remains before leaving the fort by its south-western entrance to another information board below. Go down the stony path through heather. At a path junction by a small post follow the path ahead to a kissing gate in the wall.

4 Keep ahead, past a waymarked side path, then about 100 yards further, take the next path on the left to the northern end of the small rocky ridge of Caergribin. The path then bends right and climbs onto small crags. Return down the path and just before a line of boulders, turn LEFT along a sketchy path, soon bending left beneath a large crag, then splitting. Here turn RIGHT past another small crag, then follow a good path, keeping with its left fork and soon bending right, to a kissing gate. Follow the path ahead down to a stream, then a wide green path angling RIGHT to a waymarked path junction. Turn RIGHT up the hillside. The path rises steadily past other cross-paths, later levelling out at a crossroad of paths at a waymark post where you are joined by Walk B. Turn LEFT and follow the increasingly wide path down to the multi-finger post.

when its defences were strengthened and more huts built. It was abandoned in 4 AD.

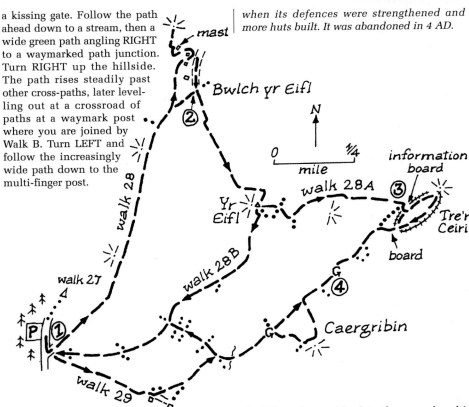

WALK 29
TRE'R CEIRI

DESCRIPTION A 4 mile walk to Tre'r Ceiri, one of the best preserved and most spectacular hillforts in Britain, returning via the small crags of Caergribin, both providing extensive views. Allow about 2½ hours.
START As Walk 26.

*T*re'r Ceiri *(Town of the Giants) Iron Age fort stands at a height of 1590 feet/485 metres. It contains an earlier Bronze Age burial cairn. The fort is encircled by a massive dry stone rampart wall, over 3 metres high, and contains the remains of over 150 round stone huts. The fort continued to be used throughout the Roman occupation,*

Follow the road back to the second multi-finger post and turn LEFT to follow the wall up across open ground, later descending with the wall to the entrance to Brynffynon cottage. Here go half-LEFT on a wide path to join a narrow green track. Follow it LEFT up to a waymarked path junction. Just beyond bend half-RIGHT up to a stream, then follow a stony path up through heather/bracken to a kissing gate. Continue with the path past a waymarked path junction to another kissing gate, then follow the path up through heather. At a path junction by a small post keep ahead up a stonier path to an information board beneath the hillfort's south-west entrance. Enter the fort and follow its massive rampart in a clockwise direction, past its impressive western entrance to complete a full interior exploration. Leave the fort and return down to the kissing gate, then follow instructions in paragraph 4 of Walk 28.

GYRN GOCH & BWLCH MAWR

DESCRIPTION A challenging 9 mile walk (**A**) exploring Llŷn's largest area of open hills and moorland, now Open Access land, offering extensive views. An alternative 6½ mile walk (**B**), which climbs up the head of the valley (1279 feet/390 metres) and avoids the hill tops is included. The route follows lane and bridleway to reach open country, then heads up the wide valley between Bwlch Mawr and Gyrn Goch. After climbing the rocky summit of Gyrn Goch (1614 feet/492 metres) it continues to a foothill of Gyrn Ddu, then descends to follow a way-marked path across moorland. After visiting several rocky tops of Bwlch Mawr (1669 feet/509 metres) the route descends to follow scenic upland roads, then a recently upgraded path to Clynnog Fawr. Allow about 6 hours. *This walk, which is mountainous in nature, is for experienced walkers and should be avoided in poor visibility.*

START Clynnog Fawr. SH 415498.

DIRECTIONS Clynnog Fawr adjoins the A499 Caernarfon-Pwllheli road. Park on a short loop section of road behind a bus shelter.

C *lynnog Fawr was an important stopping place on the pilgrimage route to Bardsey, attracted by the church first established here by the Celtic Saint St Beuno in the 7thC, which became his shrine. The current attractive 15thC church is worth a visit.*

From an information board by a post and telephone box near the former of Y Beuno pub (1912) go up the lane opposite past cottages. After a cattle grid, where it bends and becomes two stony tracks, take the sign-posted bridleway angling back up through bracken to a bridle-gate and on up to a gate. The bridleway rises to two further gates near a cottage/bunkhouse complex, then continues enclosed to a long cottage with a water-wheel. The bridleway rises between boundaries to a gate then goes up a field edge and through a gateway just before a ruin and a gate higher up. The walled bridleway rises to a bridle/kissing gate into Open Access land. Bear RIGHT to follow a path above the wall across the lower western slopes of Bwlch Mawr, shortly passing woodland.

2 At the wall corner, the route splits. (For **Walk B** continue ahead up the wide valley, keeping to the higher drier ground to pass beneath stone sheepfolds, then work your way across to join the wall rising up the head of the valley to its end at point 3.) For **Walk A**, head half-RIGHT to the bank overlooking the stream and a stone sheep-fold. Cross the stream and go up the slope to a path/track. Follow it LEFT, then take the right fork. After 20 yards follow a faint path up the eastern slopes of Gyrn Goch to a distinctive pile of stones. Now work your way up the increasingly steeper slope to the impressive rocky summit. Follow the wall descending south west. *Ahead is rocky Gyrn Ddu.* At the wall corner bear LEFT up to the top of an unnamed peak (P) . Cross the facing wall corner, then large boulders and follow the wall south down to the bottom corner. Turn LEFT along the waymarked path, rising steadily. After a ladder-stile, follow the walled path up to its end.

3 Continue east up the good path, with the wall on your right, across the moorland, guided by waymark posts, to a ladder-stile/gate in the wall ahead. Follow the path to cross another ladder-stile. (For **Walk B**, continue ahead down the path, shortly bending half-LEFT, then continuing to a ladder-stile in the wall ahead at point 4.) For **Walk A**, follow the wall LEFT to its corner. Climb through the boulders above, then go up towards a large dome-shaped boulder-covered top (**A**), passing its left-hand side. Follow a clear path half-LEFT to pass the left-hand side of Bwlch Mawr, then head NE. away from the nearby wall up to a facing wall across the highest point of Bwlch Mawr (with a trig point on the other side). Follow a path south to its rocky top (**B**). Retrace your steps a few yards then do a u-turn to continue south below the top's western side. After beginning to descend, bear LEFT down through boulders to reach an old wall in the plateau below. Follow it SE. to a huge

CLYNNOG FAWR

slab of rock, then climb over the stony ridge and go to another top ahead (**C**). Now head SW. towards top A and after passing another small craggy top on your left, head south down the slope, later bearing LEFT down to cross a ladder-stile in the wall.

5 After 1¼ miles, at Filltir hir, turn LEFT to follow a signposted bridleway along a no through road past Bryn Goleu and beneath two houses. After a gate turn RIGHT down a signposted path through bracken

Gyrn Goch

Bwlch Mawr

N

0   ¼
mile

Walk A

Walk B

sheepfolds

P

4 Join a path just below and follow it across the slope, shortly bending down to a gate in the fence. The path continues ahead down through boulders and bracken, bends down past a large boulder, descends through more bracken, passes above an area of boulders, crosses a stream, then descends more steeply to a step stile in the fence below. Keep ahead across a short wet reedy area then work your way down to another stile in a fence below. Go down the field to a stile by a ruined cottage. Turn LEFT up the road and on past a transmitter mast, then a side road.

to a small gate. Turn RIGHT down the next field and through a gap in a tree-topped embanked boundary to another gate. Follow the boardwalked path into the nearby field. Turn LEFT down the field edge and through reeds to a waymark post, then down through trees to a kissing gate. Cross a stony path to a small gate opposite. Keep ahead to cross a stream. Turn LEFT and follow the path through trees near the stream, soon descending past small falls. After emerging from the trees turn LEFT across the stream to a small gate. At a white-topped post ahead turn RIGHT down a path to a kissing gate. Follow the enclosed path to a road junction by a housing estate. Turn LEFT and follow the surfaced path opposite to join your outward road near the start.

PRONUNCIATION

These basic points should help non-Welsh speakers

Welsh	English equivalent
c	always hard, as in cat
ch	as on the Scottish word loch
dd	as th in then
f	as in of
ff	as in off
g	always hard as in got
ll	no real equivalent. It is like 'th' in then, but with an 'L' sound added to it, giving 'thlan' for the pronunciation of the Welsh 'Llan'.

In Welsh the accent usually falls on the last-but-one syllable of a word.

KEY TO THE MAPS

- → Walk route and direction
- ▬ Main road
- ▬ ▬ Minor road
- ++++ Fence
- •••• Path
- ∿→ River/stream
- Forest/woods
- ⌒ Rocks
- **G** Gate
- **S** Stile
- **F.B.** Footbridge
- ⁄⁄ Viewpoint
- ʍ Summit
- **P** Parking
- **i** Tourist Information

Published by **Kittiwake Books Limited**
3 Glantwymyn Village Workshops, Glantwymyn, Machynlleth, Montgomeryshire SY20 8LY
© Text & map research: David Berry 2014
www.davidberrywalks.co.uk
© Maps & illustrations: Kittiwake 2014
Drawings by Morag Perrott
Cover photos: *Main* – Mynydd y Graig, Walk 11.
Inset – Iron Man sculpture on Mynydd Tir-y-cwmwd, Walk 5. David Berry.
Care has been taken to be accurate.
However neither the author nor the publisher can accept responsibility for any errors which may appear, or their consequences. If you are in any doubt about access, check before you proceed.
First edition: 2007. New edition: 2014.
Printed by Mixam, UK.
ISBN: 978 **1 908748 16 4**

THE COUNTRYSIDE CODE

- Be safe – plan ahead and follow any signs
- Leave gates and property as you find them
- Protect plants and animals, and take your litter home
- Keep dogs under close control
- Consider other people

Open Access
Some routes cross areas of land where walkers have the legal right of access under The CRoW Act 2000 introduced in May 2005. Access can be subject to restrictions and closure for land management or safety reasons for up to 28 days a year. Details from: www.naturalresourceswales.gov.uk.
Please respect any notices.

About the author David Berry

David is an experienced walker with a love of the countryside and an interest in local history. He is the author of a series of walks guidebooks covering North Wales, where he has lived and worked for many years. He has written for Walking Wales magazine, worked as a Rights of Way surveyor across North Wales and served as a member of his Local Access Forum.

Whether on a riverside ramble, mountain or long distance walk, he greatly appreciates the beauty, culture and history of the landscape and hopes that his comprehensive guidebooks will encourage people to explore on foot its diverse scenery and rich heritage. For more information visit www.davidberrywalks.co.uk